land light

dave butcher

thanks

Steven Brierley and Ilford Photo/Harman Technology for their continued support in many ways but especially for providing paper and chemicals for new print lectures without which they are too expensive to do.

Long standing friends, too numerous to mention, made while working for Unilever at the Frythe Lab in the 1970s, who we walk the hills with every year. Many of the images included here are from these trips.

Al Hardacre, also a friend from Unilever days, for what has become our annual trek. It started with me going along with him as navigator for my version of the West Highland Way in 2003 (and he may still be there if I hadn't agreed to go!). This turned into our own unique Glasgow to Cape Wrath trek spread over 3 years, 330 miles and included climbing 26 mountains en route. Quite a few treks later we are still going strong and I take lots of photos on them.

prints and further information

Prints of the photographs in Land Light, and many other places, as well as further information are available from my business web site www.davebutcher.co.uk

Visit www.darkroomdave.com for free technical information.

land light
landscapes around the world
dave butcher

Published in the UK by
Dave Butcher Photography
Briarwood,
Tunstead Milton,
Whaley Bridge,
High Peak,
Derbyshire,
SK23 7ER
www.davebutcher.co.uk
©2015 Dave Butcher Photography.

British Library Cataloguing-in-Publication Data:
A catalogue record for this book is available from the British Library.

ISBN: 978-0-9555627-4-7
First edition 2015

Design and editorial production by 10th Planet.

Printed by Loop Print.

contents

introduction

This is the sister volume to Snow Light - both are books of my landscapes published at the same time. Land Light includes landscapes and coastal views without snow. Snow Light is a collection of my snowy landscapes.

Land Light starts in England, Wales and Scotland, followed by Europe, New Zealand and America. Mostly I have selected images that have a natural feel to them and are without people or intrusive buildings wherever possible. Medieval castles in the landscape are an obvious but magnificent exception to the no buildings rule!

I have included an article about producing prints as a film photographer in a digital age. This covers how I take my photographs, process my films, print in the darkroom, scan my negatives to a digital file and edit with Photoshop to roughly match what I can produce in the darkroom from negatives.

Dave Butcher, January 2015

4. Berwick Upon Tweed Beach and Moon

england | northumberland

5. Berwick Beach Reflections and Lighthouse

6. Dunstanburgh Castle Rocks

england | northumberland

7. Dunstanburgh Castle Rock Pool

8. St Mary's Lighthouse and Posts at High Tide, Whitley Bay

9. Bamburgh Castle and Waves

10. Lindisfarne Castle and Posts

11. Bamburgh Castle and Sand Dunes

england | northumberland

12. Alnwick Castle and Bridge Arch

13. Sycamore Gap, Hadrians Wall

14. Limestone Pavement and Tree at Conistone #1, Grassington

england | yorkshire

15. Kisdon Force Upper Falls, Keld

16. Wharfedale Loup Scar, Grassington

17. Wain Wath Lower Falls and Rock Pool, Keld

18. Pecca Falls, Ingleton

19. Brimham Rocks and Tree, Pateley Bridge

20. Appletreewick Hill View, Grassington

england | yorkshire

21. West Burton Waterfall, near Hawes

22. The Strid Waterfall, Grassington

23. Limestone Pavement and Tree at Conistone #2, Grassington

24. Scafell Range from Hardknott Roman Fort, Eskdale

25. Scafell Pike and Wast Water

england | lake district

26. Scafell Pike From Broad Crag

27. Wasdale from Great Gable, Infrared

28. Wast Water Reflections

29. Buttermere Fence View

england | lake district

30. Scafell Range from Harter Fell, Eskdale

31. Stanley Ghyll Force and Stream, Eskdale

32. Ritson's Force, Wasdale

33. Red Tarn and Beyond from Helvellyn

england | lake district

34. Striding Edge in Summer

35. Goyt Valley Falls
and Ferns, Buxton

england | peak district

36. Bole Hill Millstones, Hathersage

37. Goyt Valley Stakeside Falls, Buxton

38. Lumsdale Falls, Matlock

39. Cheshire Tree and Furrows, Dunham, Infrared

england | cheshire

40. St Benet's Windmill and Yacht, Thurne

41. River Thurne and Windmill at Thurne

england | norfolk

42. Seven Sisters, Eastbourne

43. Durdle Door, Dorchester

england

44. St Michaels Mount from the Causeway, Penzance

45. Brighton West Pier Ruins and Waves

46. Farley Water at Watersmeet, Lynton

england | devon

47. Snowdon from Llynau Mymbyr, Capel Curig

48. Watkin Path Waterfalls, Snowdon, Infrared

49. Tryfan from Glyder Fach

wales | snowdonia

50. Stones of Stenness Skyscape, Orkney

51. Tobermory Harbour, Mull

scotland

52. Ring of Brodgar Stones, Orkney

53. Hoxa Head Seascape and Yacht, Orkney

54. Old Man of Hoy, Orkney

55. Ettrick Bay Wreck, Bute

scotland

56. Goat Fell View Northwest, Arran

57. Finlaggan Reflections, Islay

58. Paps of Jura Reflection

59. Black Cuillin Ridge from Bruach na Frith, Skye

60. Lower Glen Coe Waterfalls

61. Glencoe Lochan Reflections

62. Glen Coe Aonach Eagach Ridge

scotland

63. Sandwood Bay

64. Suilven Reflection in Cam Loch

65. Suilven Summit Ridge

66. Clouds on Monte Perdido from Pimene, Pyrenees

67. Mont Blanc from La Tete au Vents

france

68. Lago di Landro Reflections, Misurina

69. Grandes Jorasses Reflections from Mont de la Saxe

70. Mont Blanc Prayer Flags from Tete Entre Deux Sauts

italy

71. Cime Cadin di San Lucano from below Forcella de la Neve, Misurina

72. Tre Cime di Lavaredo Reflections, Misurina

73. Cima Ambrizolla from Forcella Ambrizolla, Cortina

italy | dolomites

74. Monte Pelmo from Forcella de Formin, Cortina

75. Val de Rinbianco Tree, Misurina

76. Marmolada from Nuvolau, Cortina

77. Col Toron View and Bird, Sella

78. Simmenfalle, Lenk, Alpine Pass Route

switzerland

79. Wetterhorn Avalanche, Grindelwald, Alpine Pass Route

80. Reichenbach Falls, Meiringen, Alpine Pass Route

81. Aesch Waterfall and River, Altdorf, Alpine Pass Route

82. Matterhorn from Findeln, Zermatt

83. Foo Pass View West, Alpine Pass Route

switzerland

84. Upper Gertelbach Falls, Baden-Baden

85. Zugspitze Summit Ridge, Garmisch

germany

86. Hohenschwangau Castle and Autumn Trees

87. Hohenschwangau Castle and Alpsee Lake Reflections

88. Neuschwanstein Castle From Above

89. Puig de sa Rateta Summit View, Soller, Mallorca

spain

90. Windmill Reflections at Kinderdijk #5

91. Windmill Reflections at Kinderdijk

netherlands

sweden

92. Siljan Lake and Jetty, Mora

93. Moeraki Boulder

new zealand

94. Milford Sound and Mitre Peak Reflection

95. Fox Glacier and Ice

96. Mount Cook and Hooker Lake

97. Moeraki Boulder Skyscape

98. Castle Rock, Moab

99. Dead Horse Point, Moab

100. Delicate Arch, Moab

usa | utah

101. Canyonlands Green River Overlook, Moab

102. A Goblin Valley Goblin

103. Goblin Valley

104. Lake Isobel Waterfall, Brainard Lake State Park

usa | colorado

105. Grand Mesa Sky

106. Patterns in the Sand, Great Sand Dune National Park

usa | colorado

107. Sand Dune Tracks, Great Sand Dune National Park

108. Sand Dunes at Dusk, Great Sand Dune National Park

109. Pawnee Buttes Clouds, Fort Collins

110. Chilnualna Falls, Wawona

111. Half Dome and Merced River, Infrared

112. Mirror Lake Reflections, Tenaya Canyon

113. Mariposa Clothes Pin Tree, Wawona

114. Vernal Falls, Infrared

115. Yosemite Valley from Crocker Point

116. El Capitan and Tree

117. Nevada Falls

118. Yosemite Valley from Inspiration Point

Photography, Processing, Printing, Scanning and Editing

This describes how I take my photographs and print the final images. I take every photograph on film and process the films to produce negatives. I then have two options. Either, I use the negatives to make prints in the darkroom in the traditional way with silver gelatin papers through a chemical process or I scan the negatives and edit the digital file using Adobe Photoshop.

Photography Equipment

The high print quality that I need starts with using Mamiya 7 film cameras to take the photographs. These give 7 x 6cm negatives on 120 roll film, with just 10 negatives to each roll. I have been using Mamiya rangefinder cameras since 1993. There are few lenses available, all primes no zooms, and I have the 43mm, 65mm, 80mm and 150mm (divide by 2 for the equivalent lens on a full frame digital camera). The 43mm and 65mm are my most used lenses.

Metering is always with Sekonic spot meters and the camera is supported on Gitzo Mountaineer carbon fibre tripods with Manfrotto quick-release heads. I have a lightweight one for mountaineering and ski trips and a heavier, taller one for everything else.

Filters are essential for black and white film photography to compensate for the natural over-sensitive response of the silver halides in every film to blue light. I use B+W filters (light red, orange, yellow and UV as needed) and occasionally a Mamiya polarising filter.

I use just one film for everything, Ilford FP4 120 film at 125 ISO, except for infrared. For infrared I use Ilford SFX 120 infrared film at 6 ISO with Heliopan 715 filters.

Finally all of my gear is carried in a LowePro case on a shoulder harness on my front, between chest and waist height, to give instant access. The tripod is secured with a clip across the top of the case.

Photography Techniques

I use the same techniques for landscapes and cities, shooting what presents itself to me and also what appeals to me. Some shots are planned and take many years to finally achieve. I have waited up to 17 years, for example, to take 1 shot, returning several times to the location until conditions were right. Other images just present themselves and you have to be ready to capture them. I look for patterns, shapes, textures and tones and make my pictures as simple as possible. There are only shades of grey to separate what are normally different colours. I need to look beyond what my eyes see and interpret into what will be recorded by my black and white film and what I can achieve in the darkroom print.

First I see the overall picture and select the lens to use. This is an easy step as I seldom carry more than 2 lenses. Then I decide if it needs something in the foreground. If it does I look around for rocks, plants or lead-ins from the lower part of the shot to the main area. I then decide on camera height, choose which filter to use, if any, and check for and remove distractions especially at the edges of the image by moving the camera. A tripod is really helpful for this. I use a tripod for every shot I take on solid ground. Then I need a final check of the camera settings and focus to make sure the image will match my expectations. I use a small aperture like f22 if everything must be in focus, or f8 / f11 if there is nothing close to the lens. For waterfalls with streaky water (I like streaky water photos!) I use various slow shutter speeds but ¼ second is often best.

Using the correct exposure is essential. You can often make prints from poorly exposed negatives (or digital image files) but they won't have the same impact as one that is correctly exposed - something will have suffered at one end of the exposure scale or the other.

I always use my camera in fully manual mode and select the shutter speed, aperture and focus.

I use a separate spot meter rather than the one built in to the camera, it's much more accurate, and point it at suitable mid-tones or light shadows. There is no light meter able to tell you what exposure to use for sunlit snow, or even the average scene. It depends on where you point the meter and relates to an 18% grey reflectance, not an easy thing to work out under normal circumstances let alone in the mountains!

If in doubt I take more negatives with extra exposure, not less. The old adage for negative film users is to expose for the shadows (and let the highlights take care of themselves!). This is something of an over-simplification but indicates the importance of avoiding underexposing the shadow areas or there will be no detail there to print.

Lighting and weather is what really makes or breaks a shot. It is also what makes landscape photography so appealing. There is no such thing as the "definitive landscape shot" of a location. By this I mean there is always something different that can be seen. Even the most familiar scene can provide an interesting subject as the conditions change.

Landscape photography often gives you time to set up your shot. However, when the weather is changeable I work fast when the opportunity for a shot presents itself and take more shots when I find a better viewpoint than the one already in the bag.

Processing Films

I never change my film processing. Printing with modern variable contrast papers like Ilford Multigrade has removed the need to adjust processing so that negatives can be printed on fixed contrast papers. If you are interested, I use Ilford Ilfotec DDX 1+6 for 9 minutes at 20°C in Paterson processing tanks.

Darkroom Printing

I am one of a handful of Ilford Master Darkroom Printers and the only one trained by Ilford, during my 21 years working for them. Continuing to make prints the traditional way is important to me both for producing the highest quality prints and keeping the old skills going. These can be traced back to Fox Talbot in the 1830s. I run courses on film photography and darkroom printing workshops to pass on my skills to others and have made videos of the techniques that I use for my www.darkroomdave.com website.

Ilford is now the only manufacturer of top quality darkroom papers and films so I use them exclusively. I process my films, index them and make a contact print (print of actual size negatives without enlargement). Negatives are then selected to scan and put on the web site. The full details of how I process my films and make top quality fibre-based prints in the darkroom is on my website.

Scanning Negatives

My gallery website www.davebutcher.co.uk has several thousand images available to purchase as darkroom prints, all taken on film, and new images are added on a regular basis. To put them online the negatives have to be scanned to convert them to a digital file. My negatives are up to 7 x 6cm so I use a Nikon Super Coolscan 9000ED film scanner. I scan at 4000dpi and 16 bit greyscale using Vuescan software on my iMac and files are saved as TIFFs. The file size at this stage is about 220Mb.

Editing Scans

The scans are then edited in Photoshop, currently version CS6, using a Wacom Intuos 4 tablet instead of a mouse for fine tuning images.

The first thing I do is add copyright data as well as image location, date and other information using File Info. The image is rotated to correct for orientation and misalignment using the Image Rotation and Ruler tools or just manually using Image Rotation-Arbitrary. Then the Image Size is converted to printing resolution of 300dpi which increases the image size to over 90cm as the original data points are redistributed.

The brightness and contrast are then adjusted using a Curves layer to change the straight line provided by CS6 (shown on a histogram of exposure against density) to the usual S-shaped curve that is associated with traditional film negatives. This step is important to me as it ensures that whether printed directly from the negative or from the digital file the final image looks similar. The black and white points are set before adjusting the Curve by clicking and dragging the sliders at the base of the histogram while pressing the Alt key (on a Mac keyboard). Depending on the image I may use another Curves layer, created using the Quick Selection tool, to slightly darken the sky.

Finally I remove dust spots and hairs using the Spot Healing Brush (usually set to 40-ish) with Content-Aware selected (the software senses what is already in the image and tries to match it as it removes spots). The file size has now increased to around 800Mb with the extra layers.

The file is then edited for size using Image Size, Crop and Rectangular Marquee-Image-Crop tools to one of my 3 standard formats, square 70 x 70cm, panoramic 100 x 50cm and standard 70 x 50cm. Most of my images fit one of these 3 formats. The Curves layer may be re-edited after cropping to format before the file is flattened. If the file needs sharpening it is expanded to 100% and the Smart Sharpen tool is used before saving. File size is now around 100Mb, still as TIFF format.

The digital file is then converted to 20cm longest edge and a web resolution of 72dpi using Image Size and JPEG format before being added to my gallery website. File size is reduced to around 0.1Mb.

The cropped, flattened, high-resolution TIFF file can be used for printing high quality images larger than the 60 x 50cm I can print in my darkroom. Anything larger is now printed by Ilford Lab Direct (at the UK factory which makes the film and paper products) up to 120cm using a laser enlarger to expose my images onto special darkroom paper. This is then processed through the usual black and white darkroom chemical process to ensure high quality silver gelatin prints with known longevity.

The same high resolution images are also used for printing my books, magazine article illustrations and image licensing for calendars, greetings cards and fine art prints made using other techniques.

From this you should be able to appreciate that I have a strong bias to traditional techniques and materials but also embrace the modern digital age where appropriate!

technical data full details of all the photographs in this book

PLATE	LOCATION	IMAGE	DATE TAKEN	FILM	CAMERA
1 (front cover)	England	Bamburgh Castle and Waves	15-Jul-06	FP4	Mamiya 6
2 (frontispiece)	USA	Castle Rock, Moab	21-Jan-09	FP4	Mamiya 7
3 (introduction)	Wales	Snowdon from Llynau Mymbyr, Capel Curig	9-Mar-07	FP4	Mamiya 7
4	England	Berwick Upon Tweed Beach and Moon	10-Dec-11	FP4	Mamiya 7
5	England	Berwick Beach Reflections and Lighthouse	13-Apr-12	FP4	Mamiya 7
6	England	Dunstanburgh Castle Rocks	16-Jul-06	FP4	Mamiya 6
7	England	Dunstanburgh Castle Rock Pool	16-Jul-06	FP4	Mamiya 6
8	England	St Mary's Lighthouse and Posts at High Tide, Whitley Bay	15-Mar-13	FP4	Mamiya 7
9 (+front cover)	England	Bamburgh Castle and Waves	15-Jul-06	FP4	Mamiya 6
10	England	Lindisfarne Castle and Posts	15-Jul-06	FP4	Mamiya 6
11	England	Bamburgh Castle and Sand Dunes	14-Apr-12	FP4	Mamiya 7
12	England	Alnwick Castle and Bridge Arch	3-Aug-09	FP4	Mamiya 7
13	England	Sycamore Gap, Hadrians Wall	16-Jul-06	FP4	Mamiya 6
14	England	Limestone Pavement and Tree at Conistone #1, Grassington	8-May-11	FP4	Mamiya 7
15	England	Kisdon Force Upper Falls, Keld	9-Aug-12	FP4	Mamiya 7
16	England	Wharfedale Loup Scar, Grassington	2-Aug-08	FP4	Mamiya 7
17	England	Wain Wath Lower Falls and Rock Pool, Keld	8-Aug-12	FP4	Mamiya 7
18	England	Pecca Falls, Ingleton	3-Aug-97	FP4	Mamiya 6
19	England	Brimham Rocks and Tree, Pateley Bridge	16-Oct-08	FP4	Mamiya 7
20	England	Appletreewick Hill View, Grassington	2-Aug-08	FP4	Mamiya 7
21	England	West Burton Waterfall, near Hawes	8-May-11	FP4	Mamiya 7
22	England	The Strid Waterfall, Grassington	8-Aug-09	FP4	Mamiya 7
23	England	Limestone Pavement and Tree at Conistone #2, Grassington	8-May-11	FP4	Mamiya 7
24	England	Scafell Range from Hardknott Roman Fort, Eskdale	14-Mar-10	FP4	Mamiya 7
25	England	Scafell Pike and Wast Water	14-Mar-10	FP4	Mamiya 7
26	England	Scafell Pike From Broad Crag	2-Oct-14	FP4	Mamiya 7
27	England	Wasdale from Great Gable, Infrared	6-Jun-14	SFX	Mamiya 7
28	England	Wast Water Reflections	22-Mar-11	FP4	Mamiya 7
29	England	Buttermere Fence View	16-Mar-10	FP4	Mamiya 7
30	England	Scafell Range from Harter Fell, Eskdale	12-Jun-14	FP4	Mamiya 7
31	England	Stanley Ghyll Force and Stream, Eskdale	13-Mar-10	FP4	Mamiya 7
32	England	Ritson's Force, Wasdale	17-Mar-10	FP4	Mamiya 6
33	England	Red Tarn and Beyond from Helvellyn	10-Jun-14	FP4	Mamiya 7
34	England	Striding Edge in Summer	10-Jun-14	FP4	Mamiya 7

PLATE	LOCATION	IMAGE	DATE TAKEN	FILM	CAMERA
35	England	Goyt Valley Falls and Ferns, Buxton	14-Jul-12	FP4	Mamiya 7
36	England	Bole Hill Millstones, Hathersage	9-Mar-08	FP4	Mamiya 7
37	England	Goyt Valley Stakeside Falls, Buxton	16-Jul-09	FP4	Mamiya 7
38	England	Lumsdale Falls, Matlock	30-Jul-09	FP4	Mamiya 7
39	England	Cheshire Tree and Furrows, Dunham, Infrared	1-May-97	SFX	Mamiya 6
40	England	St Benet's Windmill and Yacht, Thurne	20-Apr-11	FP4	Mamiya 7
41	England	River Thurne and Windmill at Thurne	20-Apr-11	FP4	Mamiya 7
42	England	Seven Sisters, Eastbourne	25-Mar-09	FP4	Mamiya 7
43	England	Durdle Door, Dorchester	10-Nov-06	FP4	Mamiya 7
44	England	St Michaels Mount from the Causeway, Penzance	30-Mar-12	FP4	Mamiya 7
45	England	Brighton West Pier Ruins and Waves	25-Mar-09	FP4	Mamiya 7
46	England	Farley Water at Watersmeet, Lynton	12-Nov-06	FP4	Mamiya 7
47 (+introduction)	Wales	Snowdon from Llynau Mymbyr, Capel Curig	9-Mar-07	FP4	Mamiya 7
48	Wales	Watkin Path Waterfalls, Snowdon, Infrared	8-Jun-03	SFX	Mamiya 6
49	Wales	Tryfan from Glyder Fach	13-Sep-87	FP4	Mamiya 645
50	Scotland	Stones of Stenness Skyscape, Orkney	18-Jun-12	FP4	Mamiya 7
51	Scotland	Tobermory Harbour, Mull	1-Jun-96	FP4	Mamiya 6
52	Scotland	Ring of Brodgar Stones, Orkney	17-Jun-12	FP4	Mamiya 7
53	Scotland	Hoxa Head Seascape and Yacht, Orkney	18-Jun-12	FP4	Mamiya 7
54	Scotland	Old Man of Hoy, Orkney	20-Jun-12	FP4	Mamiya 7
55	Scotland	Ettrick Bay Wreck, Bute	29-Apr-06	FP4	Mamiya 6
56	Scotland	Goat Fell View Northwest, Arran	23-Apr-06	FP4	Mamiya 6
57	Scotland	Finlaggan Reflections, Islay	25-Apr-06	FP4	Mamiya 6
58	Scotland	Paps of Jura Reflection	25-Apr-06	FP4	Mamiya 6
59	Scotland	Black Cuillin Ridge from Bruach na Frith, Skye	11-Aug-99	FP4	Mamiya 6
60	Scotland	Lower Glen Coe Waterfalls	22-Sep-12	FP4	Mamiya 7
61	Scotland	Glencoe Lochan Reflections	23-Sep-12	FP4	Mamiya 7
62	Scotland	Glen Coe Aonach Eagach Ridge	22-Sep-12	FP4	Mamiya 7
63	Scotland	Sandwood Bay	4-Jun-05	FP4	Mamiya 6
64	Scotland	Suilven Reflection in Cam Loch	31-May-05	FP4	Mamiya 6
65	Scotland	Suilven Summit Ridge	31-May-05	FP4	Mamiya 6
66	France	Clouds on Monte Perdido from Pimene, Pyrenees	6-Sep-02	FP4	Mamiya 6
67	France	Mont Blanc from La Tete au Vents	9-Sep-04	FP4	Mamiya 6
68	Italy	Lago di Landro Reflections, Misurina	2-Oct-07	FP4	Mamiya 7
69	Italy	Grandes Jorasses Reflections from Mont de la Saxe	5-Sep-04	FP4	Mamiya 6
70	Italy	Mont Blanc Prayer Flags from Tete Entre Deux Sauts	5-Sep-04	FP4	Mamiya 6
71	Italy	Cime Cadin di San Lucano from below Forcella de la Neve, Misurina	11-Sep-11	FP4	Mamiya 7
72	Italy	Tre Cime di Lavaredo Reflections, Misurina	9-Sep-11	FP4	Mamiya 7
73	Italy	Cima Ambrizolla from Forcella Ambrizolla, Cortina	10-Sep-11	FP4	Mamiya 7
74	Italy	Monte Pelmo from Forcella de Formin, Cortina	10-Sep-11	FP4	Mamiya 7
75	Italy	Val de Rinbianco Tree, Misurina	9-Sep-11	FP4	Mamiya 7
76	Italy	Marmolada from Nuvolau, Cortina	3-Oct-07	FP4	Mamiya 7
77	Italy	Col Toron View and Bird, Sella	5-Oct-07	FP4	Mamiya 7
78	Switzerland	Simmenfalle, Lenk, Alpine Pass Route	2-Sep-06	FP4	Mamiya 7
79	Switzerland	Wetterhorn Avalanche, Grindelwald, Alpine Pass Route	3-Sep-13	FP4	Mamiya 7
80	Switzerland	Reichenbach Falls, Meiringen, Alpine Pass Route	12-Sep-13	FP4	Mamiya 7
81	Switzerland	Aesch Waterfall and River, Altdorf, Alpine Pass Route	14-Sep-13	FP4	Mamiya 7
82	Switzerland	Matterhorn from Findeln, Zermatt	21-Jul-89	FP4	Mamiya 645

PLATE	LOCATION	IMAGE	DATE TAKEN	FILM	CAMERA
83	Switzerland	Foo Pass View West, Alpine Pass Route	6-Sep-13	FP4	Mamiya 7
84	Germany	Upper Gertelbach Falls, Baden-Baden	28-Sep-07	FP4	Mamiya 7
85	Germany	Zugspitze Summit Ridge, Garmisch	6-Sep-11	FP4	Mamiya 7
86	Germany	Hohenschwangau Castle and Autumn Trees	29-Sep-07	FP4	Mamiya 7
87	Germany	Hohenschwangau Castle and Alpsee Lake Reflections	30-Sep-07	FP4	Mamiya 7
88	Germany	Neuschwanstein Castle From Above	30-Sep-07	FP4	Mamiya 7
89	Spain	Puig de sa Rateta Summit View, Soller, Mallorca	26-Nov-01	FP4	Mamiya 6
90	Netherlands	Windmill Reflections at Kinderdijk #5	22-Sep-09	FP4	Mamiya 7
91	Netherlands	Windmill Reflections at Kinderdijk	22-Sep-09	FP4	Mamiya 7
92	Sweden	Siljan Lake and Jetty, Mora	2-Oct-09	FP4	Mamiya 7
93	New Zealand	Moeraki Boulder	10-Nov-10	FP4	Mamiya 7
94	New Zealand	Milford Sound and Mitre Peak Reflection	9-Nov-10	FP4	Mamiya 7
95	New Zealand	Fox Glacier and Ice	5-Nov-10	FP4	Mamiya 7
96	New Zealand	Mount Cook and Hooker Lake	12-Nov-10	FP4	Mamiya 7
97	New Zealand	Moeraki Boulder Skyscape	10-Nov-10	FP4	Mamiya 7
98 (+frontispiece)	USA	Castle Rock, Moab	21-Jan-09	FP4	Mamiya 7
99	USA	Dead Horse Point, Moab	20-Jan-09	FP4	Mamiya 7
100	USA	Delicate Arch, Moab	19-Jan-09	FP4	Mamiya 7
101	USA	Canyonlands Green River Overlook, Moab	20-Jan-09	FP4	Mamiya 7
102	USA	A Goblin Valley Goblin	15-Jan-09	FP4	Mamiya 7
103	USA	Goblin Valley	15-Jan-09	FP4	Mamiya 7
104	USA	Lake Isobel Waterfall, Brainard Lake State Park	13-Jul-05	FP4	Mamiya 6
105	USA	Grand Mesa Sky	10-Jul-05	FP4	Mamiya 6
106	USA	Patterns in the Sand, Great Sand Dune National Park	1-Jan-11	FP4	Mamiya 7
107 (+back cover)	USA	Sand Dune Tracks, Great Sand Dune National Park	6-Jul-05	FP4	Mamiya 6
108	USA	Sand Dunes at Dusk, Great Sand Dune National Park	5-Jul-05	FP4	Mamiya 6
109	USA	Pawnee Buttes Clouds, Fort Collins	1-Jul-05	FP4	Mamiya 6
110	USA	Chilnualna Falls, Wawona	11-May-08	FP4	Mamiya 7
111	USA	Half Dome and Merced River, Infrared	9-May-08	SFX	Mamiya 7
112	USA	Mirror Lake Reflections, Tenaya Canyon	6-May-08	FP4	Mamiya 7
113	USA	Mariposa Clothes Pin Tree, Wawona	12-May-08	FP4	Mamiya 7
114	USA	Vernal Falls, Yosemite, Infrared	7-May-08	SFX	Mamiya 7
115	USA	Yosemite Valley from Crocker Point	5-May-08	FP4	Mamiya 7
116	USA	El Capitan and Tree	6-May-08	FP4	Mamiya 7
117	USA	Nevada Falls	7-May-08	FP4	Mamiya 7
118	USA	Yosimite Valley from Inspiration Point	5-May-08	FP4	Mamiya 7
119 (back cover)	USA	Sand Dune Tracks, Great Sand Dune National Park	6-Jul-05	FP4	Mamiya 6